Megalodon:
The Largest Shark and Deadliest Predator

A.J. Miller

DEDICATION

To all those fascinated by these giant prehistoric creatures.
May you always stay curious and excited for learning.

CONTENTS

WHAT WAS MEGALODON?

Megalodon was not only the biggest shark in the world, but one of the largest fish to ever exist! Estimates suggest it grew to between 15 and 18 meters in length. That's approximately 60 - 70 feet, three times longer than the largest great white shark and about the same size as a semi-truck!

Scientists were able to predict the massive size of this shark from its teeth, the largest megalodon tooth found measured 18 centimeters, around 7 inches. That's three times longer than teeth from a great white shark.

The name name megalodon is Ancient Greek for "big tooth" which considering their size makes perfect sense.

WHEN AND WHERE DID MEGALODON LIVE?

The earliest megalodon fossils date to about 20 million years ago and they lived for around 13 million years after that as the largest predators in the oceans. The time period they were alive is known as the Early Miocene to the Pliocene.

They went extinct only about 3.6 million years ago. Scientists determined this by examining their fossils and discovering that until that time there had been a continuous fossil record for megalodon around the west coast.

As far as where the megalodon lived a better question may be, where didn't it live! Scientists say megalodon had a cosmopolitan distribution, that means that they lived across all or most of the world!

Megalodon's fossil teeth have been found in many regions including North and South America, Europe, Africa, Puerto Rico, Cuba, Jamaica, the Canary Islands, Australia, New Zealand, Japan, Malta, Grenadines and India. In fact they have been found on every continent except Antarctica. Whew that's a lot of places!

Scientist do say that megalodon preferred subtropical to temperate waters, which is to say they liked the water anywhere as long as it was warm enough. They lived in a wide range of environments and exhibited a transient lifestyle, which means they were always on the move often traveling the ocean.

HOW LARGE WAS MEGALODON?

Since sharks are mostly cartilage (that's what your nose and ears are made of) which does not stick around like bone does (the reason why skeletons don't have noses or ears), there are no remains left of megalodon other than its teeth and vertebrae.

Due to this, the size of megalodon are estimates made by scientists based on the size of their teeth and vertebrae, and boy are those estimates big!

Scientist believe megalodon to be 15 - 18 meters or 60-70 feet and an estimated maximum weight of over 60 tons. That's about the same weight as 9 elephants! The Megalodon is the largest known predator in Earth's history. The largest modern Great White sharks are around 7 meters or 23 feet and 3 ½ tons. This makes the Megalodon nearly 3 times as long, and 20 times and heavy as the Great White Shark.

MEGALADON
MAX SIZE
MEGALADON
MINIMUM
SIZE
GREAT
WHITE

MEGALODON
GREAT WHITE

HOW BIG WERE MEGALODON'S TEETH?

Megalodon teeth size ranges anywhere from 5 centimeters (2 inches) to 18 centimeters (7 inches). If you think that's big they also had around 276 teeth in 5 rows! All sharks including megalodon produce teeth throughout their entire lives. They usually lose a set of teeth every 1 to 2 weeks, going through around 40,000 teeth in their life time, because of this there are many fossilized teeth for scientists to find.

The vast majority of megalodon fossil teeth have significant wear to the tip or the tips completely gone. This is due to hitting bone or other teeth when they are feeding on their prey.

To fit that many large teeth as well as to attack their prey, the megalodon's jaw was extremely wide. It is estimated their jaw would span 2.7 by 3.4 meters wide, thats almost 9 by 11 feet big enough to swallow two adult people standing next to each other.

Megalodon's are also believed to have the greatest bite force of any animal, biting down with the force of 108,000 - 182,000 Newtons. For context an average human has the bite force of around 1,300 Newtons, and great white sharks bit with the force of 18,000 Newtons.

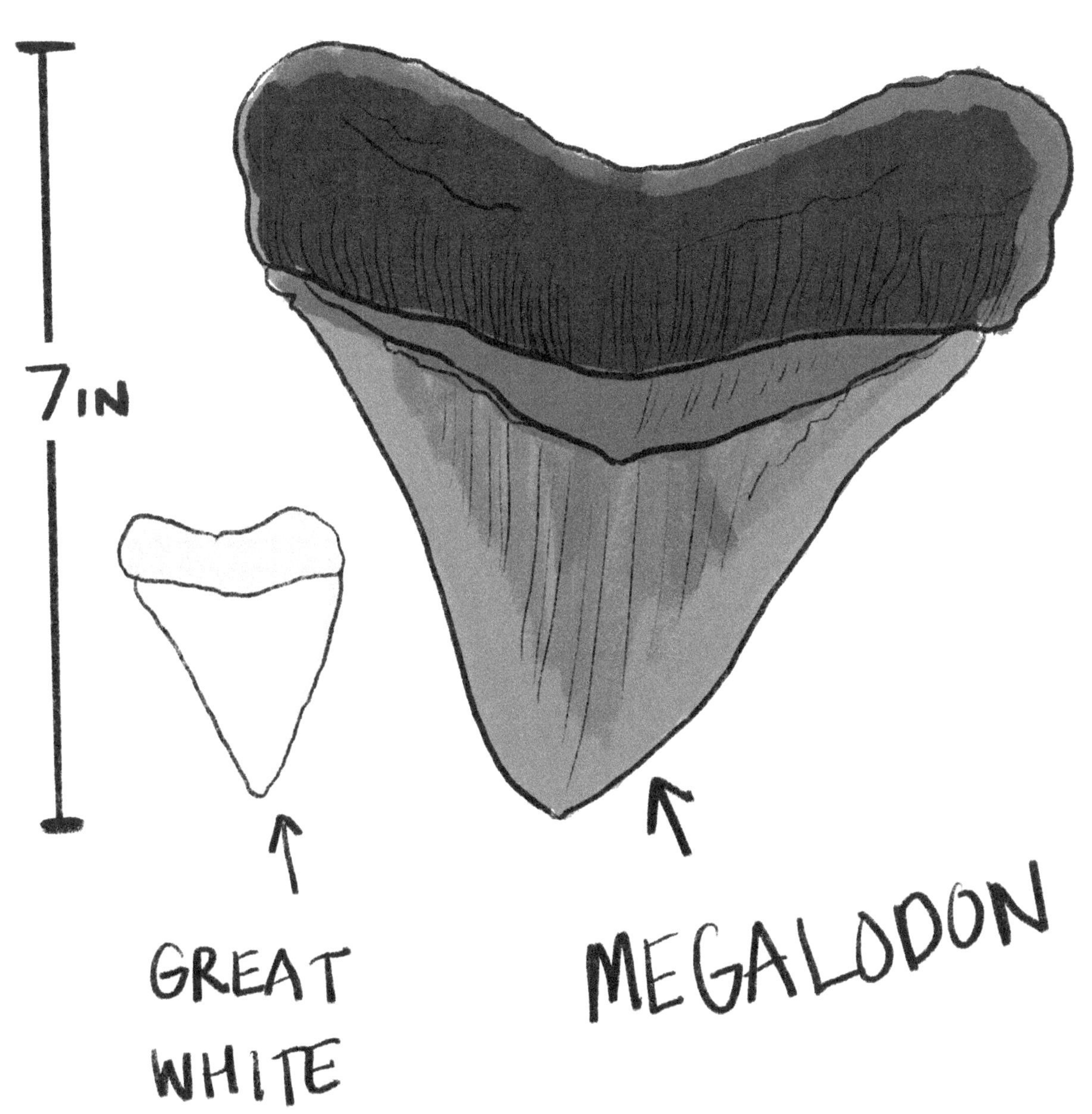

7IN
GREAT WHITE
MEGALODON

WHAT DID MEGALODON EAT?

Megalodon's large, serrated (jagged and sharp like a saw) teeth mean that they would have eaten meat. Whales, large fish, dolphins, and most likely other sharks too. Due to their massive size, megalodon would have also needed to eat a lot of food, scientists predict around a ton of food per day.

Some fossilized whale bones have been discovered with the large cut marks of megalodon teeth right on the bone. Other whale bones include the tips of megalodon teeth that were broken off during feeding.

Baby megalodon's, or pups, lived in the warm coastal waters and would have fed on fish and small whales. Megalodon pups are believed to have been the size of adult great white sharks of today. Whereas the adult megalodons would have used its strong jaws to break through it's large prey

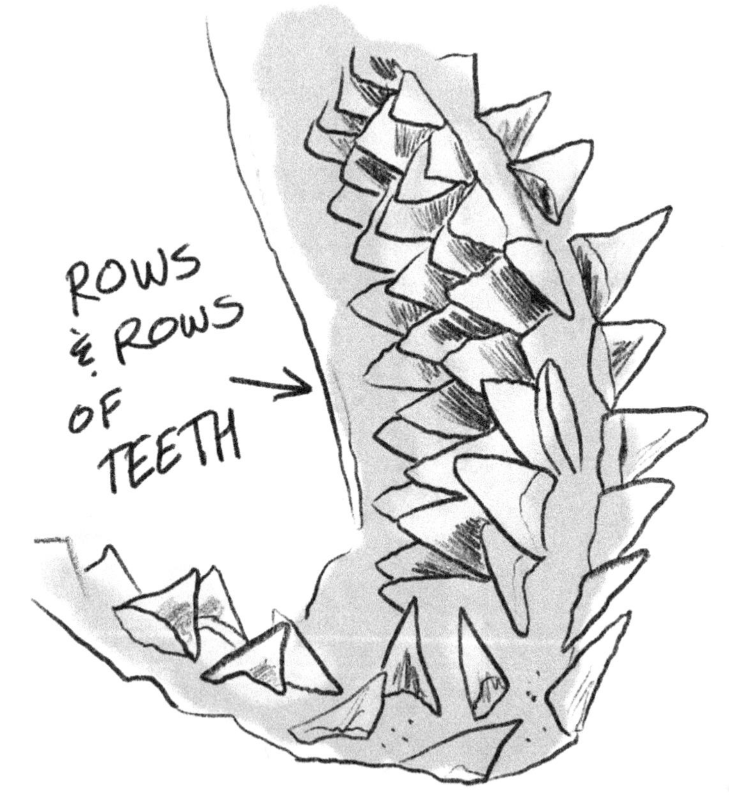

WHAT DID MEGALODON LOOK LIKE?

For a long time people believed that megalodon looked like an even larger great white shark however with new information scientists believe that is not the case.

They believe megalodon may have had a much shorter nose compared to the great white with an almost squashed looking jaw. Similar to a blue shark they believe megalodon had extra-long pectoral fins to support its great weight and size.

The reason why megalodon was thought to look like a giant great white shark is because it used to be believed that they were related. Scientists have since disproven this, megalodon is actually from a different lineage of shark known as Otodus obliquus. The evolutionary history of this shark is believed to stretch back 105 million years. This would make the lineage of megalodon over 100 million years old!

With more and more fossil evidence some scientists believe the actual ancestor to the great white shark lived alongside megalodon and some even believe they may have been in competition with each other.

WHY DID MEGALODON GO EXTINCT?

Scientists believe that the extinction of megalodon had to do with the planet cooling on a global scale. The planet cooling had a domino effect where approximately one third of all marine animals became extinct. Since megalodon was reliant on those creatures for food they would have had much less to eat and would have begun to die off.

The cooling of the oceans was also a contributing factor. Megalodon was dependent on warmer, tropical waters. With the ocean cooling, megalodon would have suffered a significant loss of habitat.

Another reason for the extinction of megalodon would be due to the fact that megalodon gave birth to its young close to shore. With ice forming at the poles and the sea level dropping the waters megalodon used for a nursery would have been destroyed.

In addition, there is newer evidence suggesting the great white shark would have started to compete for food sources leaving even less for megalodon. After the extinction of megalodon the ecosystem was affected in other ways. With the lack of the large predators the size of baleen whales increased significantly.

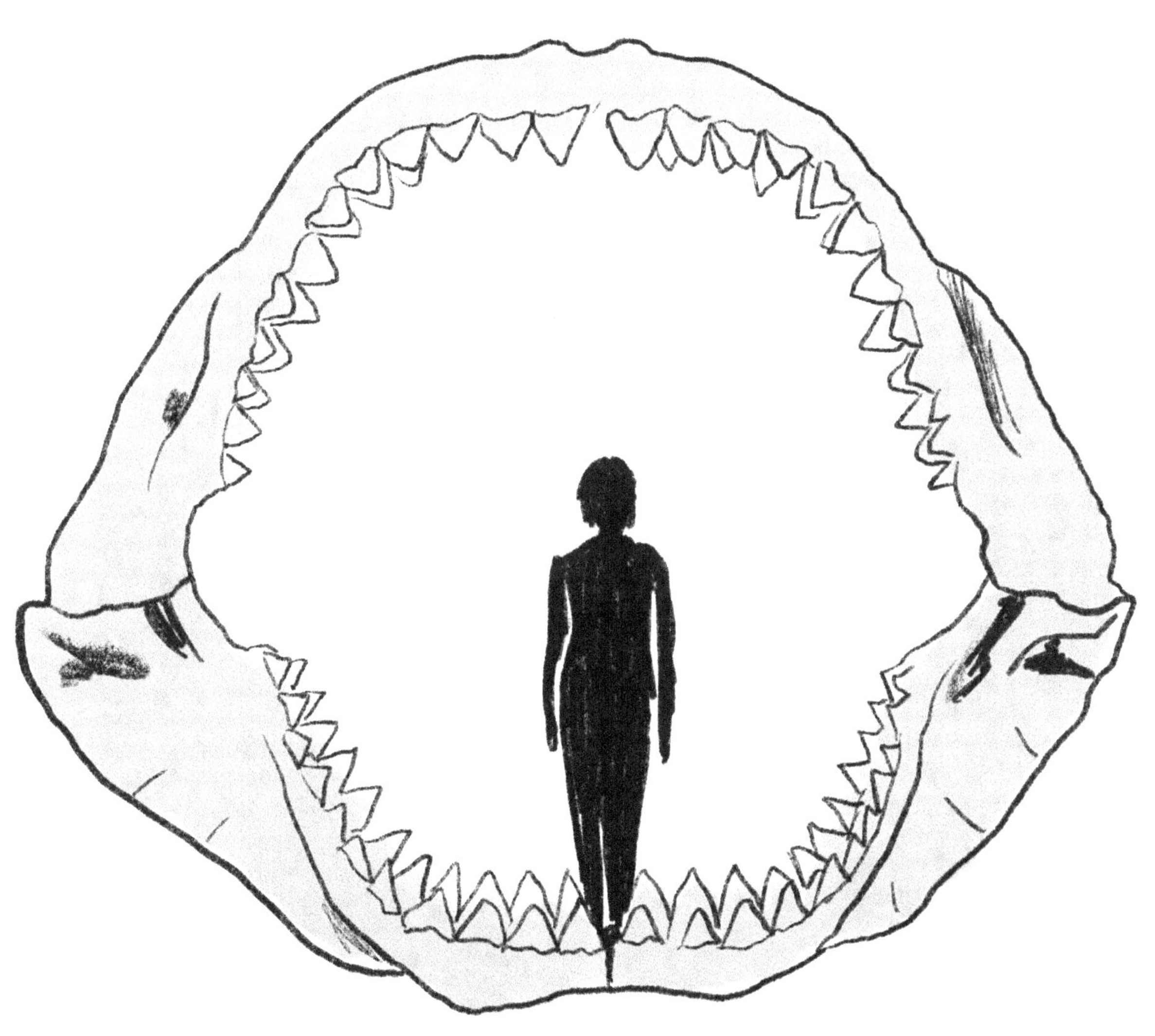

COULD MEGALODON STILL BE OUT THERE?

Don't worry the next time you're at the ocean if you are afraid of megalodon, scientists say that it is definitely not alive any longer and definitely not living in the deep ocean.

There would be substantial evidence such as bite marks on other large marine animals and their teeth would continue to be found all over the ocean floor. Neither of those things is happening. In addition, megalodon was a warm-water species, meaning it would be unable to survive unnoticed in the very cold waters of the deep ocean.

www.ingramcontent.com/pod-product-compliance
Lightning Source LLC
Chambersburg PA
CBHW080855160726
47999CB00009B/3139